W9-DDA-212

WI

The Life Cycle Series

The Life Cycle of a

Spider

Bobbie Kalman & Kathryn Smithyman

🌱 Crabtree Publishing Company

www.crabtreebooks.com

The Life Cycle Series

A Bobbie Kalman Book

Dedicated by Kathryn Smithyman
For my dear friend, Janine Armstrong

Editor-in-Chief
Bobbie Kalman

Writing team
Bobbie Kalman
Kathryn Smithyman

Editors
Niki Walker
Amanda Bishop

Copy editor
Jaimie Nathan

Cover and title page design
Campbell Creative Services

Computer design
Margaret Amy Reiach

Production coordinator
Heather Fitzpatrick

Photo researcher
Jaimie Nathan

Consultant
Patricia Loesche, Ph.D., Animal Behavior Program,
Department of Psychology, University of Washington

Photographs:
Robert McCaw: front cover, pages 3, 4, 8, 10 (top), 11 (bottom),
14, 18, 24 (top), 29 (top)
Tom Stack and Associates: Joe McDonald: page 1;
    Mark Newman: page 22 (top);
    Milton Rand: pages 12, 26-27;
    Tom Stack: page 11 (top)
James H. Robinson: pages 10 (bottom), 13, 20, 25
Frank S. Balthis: pages 21, 30
James Kamstra: pages 22 (bottom), 24 (bottom)
Bobbie Kalman: page 31
Other images by Digital Stock

Illustrations:
Tiffany Wybouw: series logo, spider border, back cover,
pages 5 (top), 17 (top), 21, 25, 30
Barbara Bedell: pages 5 (bottom), 16, 17 (bottom), 19, 23
Margaret Amy Reiach: pages 6-7, 9, 12, 14, 15 (spiderlings),
25, 28, 29
Bonna Rouse: page 15 (right)

Crabtree Publishing Company

www.crabtreebooks.com   1-800-387-7650

PMB 16A	612 Welland Avenue	73 Lime Walk
350 Fifth Avenue	St. Catharines	Headington
Suite 3308	Ontario	Oxford
New York, NY	Canada	OX3 7AD
10118	L2M 5V6	United Kingdom

Cataloging-in-Publication Data
Kalman, Bobbie
    The life cycle of a spider / Bobbie Kalman & Kathryn Smithyman.
        p. cm. -- (The life cycle series)
Includes index.
Presents information about spiders, including different species,
reproduction, differences between males and females, and some ways
to protect spiders from environmental damage.
    ISBN 0-7787-0688-5 (pbk.) -- ISBN 0-7787-0658-3 (RLB)
    1. Spiders--Life cycles--Juvenile literature. [1. Spiders.]
I. Smithyman, Kathryn II. Title.
QL458.4 .K348 2002
595.4'4--dc21
                                                    LC 2002002278

Contents

What is a spider?

Spiders are **arachnids**—they are not insects. Insects have six legs and three body sections, but arachnids have eight legs and two body sections. Arachnids have an **abdomen** and a **cephalothorax**. In the picture on the left, you can see that a spider's two body sections are joined by a tiny waist.

Hinged feet, hard cases

Both arachnids and insects are **arthropods**. The word "arthropod" means "hinged feet." All arthropods have joints that bend. Arthropods are **invertebrates**, which means they do not have backbones. Instead, arthropods have a hard outer case called an **exoskeleton**.

*Spiders are **predators**, or hunters. The crab spider above is feeding on a wasp that it has caught.*

A spider up close

The cephalothorax is a spider's head and **thorax**, or upper body. The spider's abdomen contains organs and silk glands, or **spinnerets**. All spiders make silk with their spinnerets.

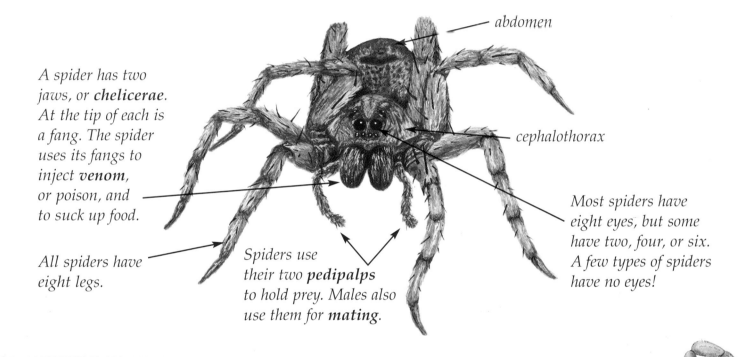

A spider has two jaws, or **chelicerae**. At the tip of each is a fang. The spider uses its fangs to inject **venom**, or poison, and to suck up food.

All spiders have eight legs.

Spiders use their two **pedipalps** to hold prey. Males also use them for **mating**.

abdomen

cephalothorax

Most spiders have eight eyes, but some have two, four, or six. A few types of spiders have no eyes!

Spider relatives

Mites, scorpions, and harvestmen, or daddy longlegs, are also arachnids.

A scorpion also has two body sections. Its abdomen has many small **segments**. The last segment on its tail is a stinger.

Mites are tiny. They look as though they have only one body section, but they have two. Many live and feed underground and among fallen leaves.

Harvestmen have tiny chelicerae. Their cephalothorax and abdomen are joined by a wide waist.

All sorts of spiders

Spiders have lived on Earth for more than 300 million years! They can be found in every part of the world except Antarctica. They live in caves, swamps, fields, and deserts. Many spiders make their homes in forests.

Scientists have identified almost 35,000 **species**, or types, of spiders. There may be thousands more that have not yet been discovered. Spiders come in a variety of sizes and colors. Only half of all spiders weave webs.

huntsman spider

jumping spider

brown recluse spider

trapdoor spider

wolf spider

crab spider

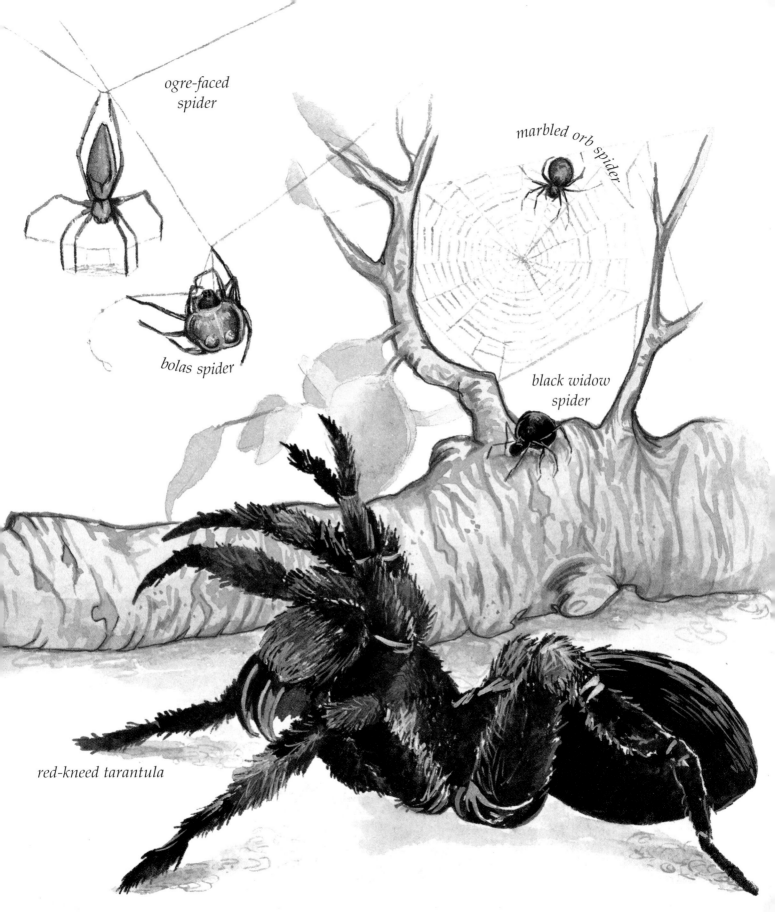

ogre-faced
spider

marbled orb spider

bolas spider

black widow
spider

red-kneed tarantula

What is a life cycle?

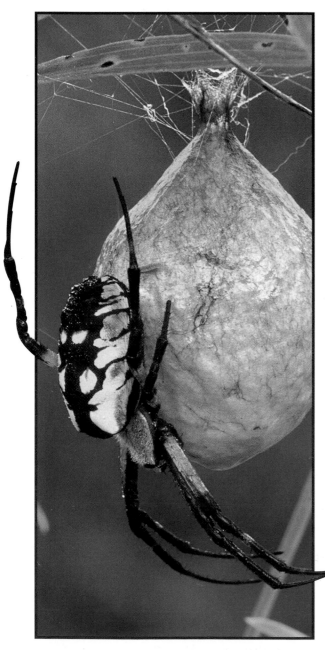

Every animal goes through a **life cycle**. A life cycle is made up of the major **stages**, or changes, in an animal's life. First, it is born or hatches from an egg. The animal then grows and changes until it becomes an adult that can make babies of its own. When an animal has babies, a new life cycle begins. All spiders go through these changes during their life cycle. Some spiders move through the stages more quickly than others, however, depending on their **life span**.

Life span

An animal's life span is the length of time it is alive. Most spiders live for one or two years. Some large spiders, such as tarantulas and trapdoor spiders, can live up to 20 years. These spiders go through their life cycles at a slower pace than smaller spiders do.

Female spiders, such as this female black-and-yellow argiope, usually live longer than male spiders do.

adult

egg sac filled
with eggs

juvenile

hatchlings

A spider's life cycle

Every spider begins its life inside an egg laid by its mother. Spider eggs are contained inside an **egg sac**. Tiny baby spiders, called **spiderlings**, hatch inside the egg sac. Soon after they hatch, the spiderlings leave the egg sac and begin to hunt for food. They become young spiders living on their own. They hunt and grow. A spider grows by **molting**, or shedding, its exoskeleton. The old covering is replaced by a larger new one. When spiders are **mature**, or adult, they look for a mate and produce babies of their own.

In the egg

Each type of spider makes a slightly different sac. Some sacs are like paper, and others are covered in a sticky mesh. A few types of sacs are very hard.

Before female spiders lay their eggs, they spin a sheet of silk. Some spiders lay just a few eggs on their sheet, but most lay thousands. They then wrap the sheet and eggs with more silk to form an egg sac.

Egg sacs

The egg sac helps shelter the eggs from the weather and from **predators**. Many types of insects and animals, including other spiders, try to eat spider eggs.

Inside the egg

Inside each egg, a **yolk** provides **nutrients**, or food energy, for the developing spider. The baby lives on these nutrients while its body grows. When the spider outgrows its egg, it hatches.

Spider eggs are tiny and round. Most are only $\frac{1}{25}$ inch (1 mm) across!

Keeping eggs safe

Most spiders do not guard their eggs.
They protect the eggs in other ways.
Many web-weaving spiders hang
their egg sacs from leaves or
branches to hide them and keep
them out of reach of predators.
Spiders that do not weave webs
bury their egg sacs or hide them
under leaves or rocks. Spiders
that live in **burrows**, or holes in
the ground, keep their sacs there.
Wolf spiders and fishing spiders,
shown below, protect their egg
sacs by attaching them
to their bodies.

*The black widow lays many eggs. She wraps
them in several layers of silk.*

fishing spider

Hatching spiderlings

Spiderlings are ready to hatch a few weeks after the eggs are laid. They break their eggs using a small, sharp growth near the base of their palps. This growth falls off after a while. The tiny spiders do not have any color yet, and their bodies are not fully formed. They cannot move around or eat, so they continue to live off their yolks. They stay inside the egg sac to grow a little more, and they molt once or twice before they are ready to leave the sac. The garden spiderlings shown above have developed their color and are nearly ready to leave the sac.

On hold

Spiders that live in cold areas can put their life cycles on hold. This pause, or break, in development is called **diapause**. If spiders lay their eggs in autumn, the tiny spiders inside the eggs will not start to develop until the warm weather arrives in the spring. Spiderlings that are still inside the egg sac when autumn arrives also wait until spring before they continue developing.

These black widow spiderlings will stay clustered together until they are large and strong enough to leave the egg sac.

A little time with Mom

Most spiderlings stay together for the first few days after they leave their sacs. Many are on their own, without a mother. A few species of spiders care for their spiderlings, however. These mothers feed and protect their spiderlings in a silk nest. They share their food with the babies until the spiderlings are big enough to live and hunt on their own.

Newly hatched wolf spiderlings crawl onto their mother's body. She protects and feeds them for about ten days.

Scattering spiders

Most spiders live together only during the time that they are in the egg sac. They are predators, so as soon as they are able to hunt, they become a threat to one another. They must **disperse**, or scatter, to avoid being eaten! Some types of spiderlings disperse just a few days after leaving the egg sac, whereas others stay together for a couple weeks before going off on their own. When spiderlings first feed on their own, they often eat tiny insects. Window lace-weaver spiderlings eat their mother's body as their first meal!

These garden spiderlings scatter soon after they hatch. Some are so hungry that they eat a few of their brothers and sisters before they leave!

Blown off

Some spiderlings leave their egg sac by **ballooning**, or traveling through the air. To balloon, a spiderling balances on two legs, lifts its abdomen, and shoots a thin strand of silk into the air. The wind catches the silk and pulls the spiderling off its perch. In the spring, thousands of young spiders can be seen flying through the air! Not all spiderlings balloon away from their egg sacs. Many types of spiderlings simply crawl away to start life on their own.

Spiders that disperse by ballooning end up in several areas. Some are carried far away from their place of birth. Where do you think these baby spiders might land?

Shedding their coats

A spiderling's hard exoskeleton cannot stretch or grow along with the spider. The spiderling must molt its old exoskeleton in order to get bigger. It saves its energy for molting by eating very little and by staying still.

Molting can take from fifteen minutes to a whole day! When a spider sheds its old case, a soft new exoskeleton is waiting underneath. The new exoskeleton takes a while to harden. Until it does, the spider has time to grow.

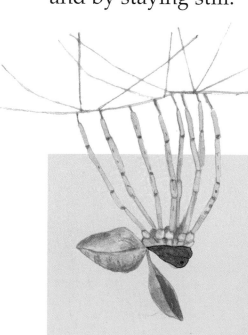

To molt, a web-weaving spider hangs from a strand of silk. Its body fills with fluid, and its exoskeleton splits along the edge of the cephalothorax.

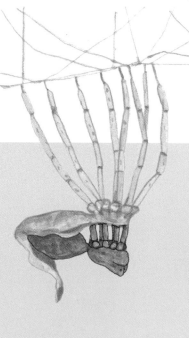

As the exoskeleton splits farther along the abdomen, the spider begins to wiggle its legs and pull them out of the old skin.

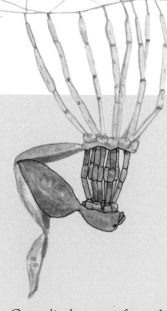

Once its legs are free, the spider dangles until its new exoskeleton hardens. The spider then climbs up and over the empty case to the web.

Watch it!

A spider must be very careful when it frees itself from its old exoskeleton. Its soft body is so fragile that if one of its legs got stuck, the spider could accidentally pull it off! If a spider loses a leg during a molt, it might **regenerate**, or grow another leg, at its next molt. If the spider loses a leg during its last molt, however, it is out of luck—and a leg!

Spiders that do not build webs, such as this red-kneed tarantula, lie on their backs to molt. Spiders with long life spans replace their worn-out exoskeletons by continuing to molt even after they have stopped growing.

A risky time

Without its hard skin, the spider's body is soft and pale. Being without an exoskeleton is very dangerous for the spider because it has no protection against predators. Until the new exoskeleton dries and hardens, the spider cannot move, eat, or defend itself. If a predator finds the spider while its skin is still soft, it can easily eat the spider. The huntsman spider on the left has safely finished molting and scurries away, leaving its old exoskeleton behind.

All grown up

A spider becomes an adult when it finishes growing and is able to make babies. Small spiders with short life spans become adults within a few weeks of hatching.

Larger spiders that live a long time can take up to ten years to become fully grown. Male spiders become adults sooner than females do.

The male bowl-and-doily spider on the left is smaller than the female on the right.

Males and females

In most species, adult female spiders look very different from the males. The females are usually much bigger and have large abdomens. Males tend to be small and more colorful.

The female black widow is a giant compared to her mate! Her large abdomen stores a lot of eggs.

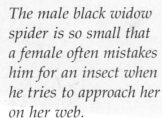

The male black widow spider is so small that a female often mistakes him for an insect when he tries to approach her on her web.

Making babies

*This male spider plucks the female's web to make **vibrations**, or movements, that the female will recognize before he approaches her.*

As soon as spiders are mature, they start to seek out a mate. Most adult spiders are **solitary**, which means they live alone. The only time spiders get together is to mate.

Planning ahead

The male spider prepares to mate even before he has found a partner. First, he makes a small web and puts a drop of **sperm** from his body on the silk threads. Sperm is the liquid that **fertilizes** a female's eggs so that babies can grow inside them. The male then sucks up the sperm with the tips of his palps, which have special holders for the liquid. His palps are now **charged**, and the spider is ready to head off to find a female.

Searching high and low

A male spider must leave his usual hiding places to wander in search of a female. He often finds a mate by following the scent she leaves on her webs and **draglines** (see page 23). If you notice a spider walking around, it is probably a male spider seeking a mate. Do not touch him! If you can get a good look, try to see if the spider really is a male by looking for its big pedipalps.

Careful courting

A male web-weaver approaches a female cautiously so that she will not mistake him for prey. Males of different species have various ways of letting females know that they are approaching to mate and not to be eaten. Some males pluck the web in a certain way. Others present the female with a gift of food wrapped in silk and then mate with her while she is distracted.

Look at me!

This male spider is searching for a female. His palps are full of sperm. Some male ground spiders wave their palps or perform courting dances to attract a female.

A male spider's pedipalps have sacs to hold sperm.

Spinning silk

A funnel-web spider hides in the tube at the center of its web, which traps insects.

Burrows help spiders hide from enemies and offer shelter from the weather.

All spiders spin silk, whether or not they build webs. Silk is important to their survival. Spiders protect their eggs with silk, and they also use it to make homes and catch prey. You can read more about hunting on pages 24-25.

Home, silk home

Spiders use silk to build their homes. Some spin webs on which they will live. Others live in silk tunnels surrounded by webs. Tarantulas and other large spiders usually live in underground burrows. They line their burrows with silk, which helps make the walls of the burrows stronger. Many spiders hide the burrow entrance with a silk sheet.

Lifelines

Many spiders trail
out a line of silk,
called a dragline,
as they walk from
place to place. If the
spider falls or jumps away
from an enemy, it uses its dragline
just as a mountain-climber uses a
safety line to prevent a fall. The spider
hangs from the line and then climbs
up it again after the danger has passed.

Making silk

There are seven types of spider silk, but no spider can
make all seven kinds. A spider makes silk in its abdomen.
The silk is a liquid when it is inside the spider's body.
The spider squeezes it out through its spinnerets.
As the liquid leaves the spider's body, it dries into
a stretchy line of silk. The spider tugs the line as the
silk leaves the spinnerets. The harder it pulls, the
stronger the silk becomes. Spider silk is one of the
strongest materials in the world for its size. If a strand
of silk were the size of a pencil, it would be stronger
than a steel post of the same size!

23

Catching food

Orb webs hang between branches and snag any insects that fly into them.

This spider blends in with the tree trunk on which it rests. Its prey does not see it—until it is too late!

Spiders are fierce predators. They feed mainly on insects such as ants, bees, wasps, beetles, moths, butterflies, and grasshoppers. Some even attack and eat other spiders! Large spiders eat birds, mice, lizards, frogs, snakes, and fish.

Well-made webs

About half of all spiders spin webs to trap prey. Some spiders weave webs between leaves or branches, where flying insects do not see them until it is too late. The insects become tangled and cannot escape. Other spiders weave thick webs that are like sheets or hammocks. They wait for an insect to land or crawl on the webs and get stuck on the sticky threads.

Gotcha!

Spiders that do not weave webs hide and surprise their prey or sneak up and grab it. Some use **camouflage**, or coloring that blends in with their surroundings, and wait for prey to come near. Others hide in their burrows and pop out to surprise their prey. Some spiders, such as the green lynx spider below, **stalk** their prey. When they sense prey nearby, they follow it until they can grab it or pounce on it. Hunting spiders have good vision. They usually have many large eyes.

The green lynx spider will soon catch and eat the jumping spider. Spiders are always on the lookout for something to eat—including another spider!

Feeding on prey

All spiders produce venom. Spiders **paralyze** their prey by biting it and shooting venom into its body through their fangs. Paralyzed prey cannot move to escape or fight back. Spiders may eat their prey right away or wrap it in silk and save it to eat later.

Many spiders, such as this argiope, hunt prey that is their size or even bigger.

Suck it up!

Spiders do not chew their food. They use special juices to **dissolve** the animal's soft body parts into a liquid. Some inject their prey with the juices, and others crunch open their prey with their jaws and spit the juice into its body. When the animal's insides become liquid, the spiders suck it up through their fangs. All that remains after the spider is finished is an empty shell!

Dangers to spiders

Spiders all over the world are in danger of losing their **habitats** as people clear natural areas to expand cities and farms. Like all animals, spiders suffer and die when their natural habitats are polluted. The world's land, water, and air is being polluted more and more by poisonous gases and toxic wastes from factories and cars.

Rainforest spiders

The millions of spiders that live in rainforests are in particular danger. Acres of rainforests are being burned to the ground every day. Scientists believe that many species of rainforest spiders have not yet been discovered. They are worried that some of these spiders may become **extinct** before we ever learn they exist! An extinct species is gone from the Earth forever.

Pesticides

Spiders eat pests that feed on plants, such as flies and insect larvae. When people spray plants and crops with pesticides to kill pests, they also poison spiders. Without spiders, many types of insects quickly return to the plants. Some farmers respond by spraying even more pesticides, which can kill off spider populations and harm all animals.

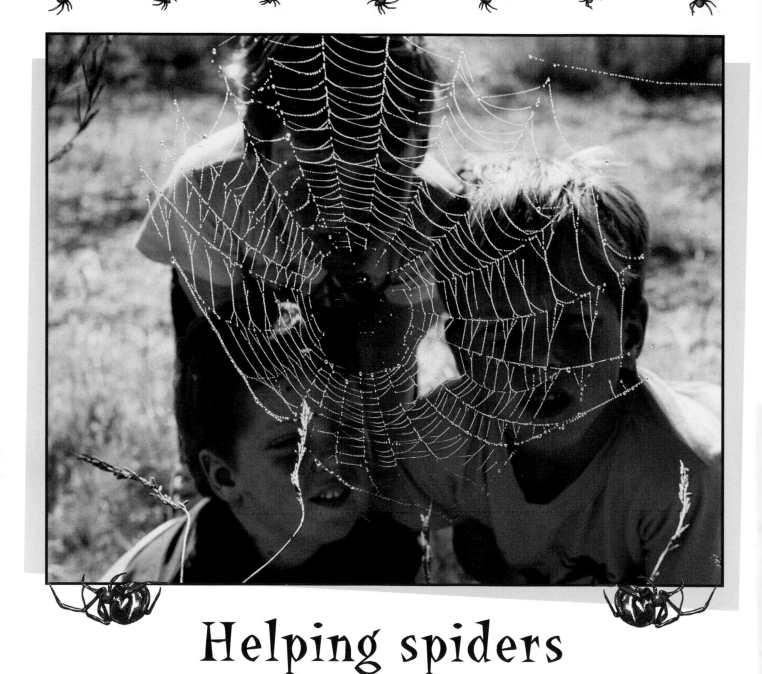

Helping spiders

If you are afraid of spiders, you are not alone! Many people fear spiders because of their venom or because they look fearsome.

Spiders are an important part of the natural world, and people need to learn about and observe spiders in order to overcome their fears.

Learn about spiders

Spider venom is poisonous, but it is deadly only to the other spiders, insects, and animals upon which spiders prey. Very few spiders are large enough or have enough venom to hurt a human. If you live in an area where large poisonous spiders live, learn about their behaviors and avoid the spiders as much as possible.

Valuable venom

Researchers use spider venom to develop cures for poisonous spider bites. These **antivenins** make living near poisonous spiders much safer. Some scientists are also using spider toxins to make other medicines. They believe spider toxins can be used to help humans who suffer from illnesses such as cancer and heart disease.

Glossary

abdomen The part of an arachnid's body that contains its major organs

antivenin A liquid containing tiny amounts of spider venom that is used to treat dangerous spider bites

cephalothorax The joined head and upper body of an arachnid

dissolve To turn into liquid

dragline A line of silk that a spider attaches to a secure place, which allows the spider to jump or drop away safely

egg sac A soft pouch in which eggs are laid

fertilize To add sperm to an egg so a baby can form inside

habitat The natural place where a plant or animal is found

mate To join together to make babies

predator An animal that hunts and kills other animals

stalk To follow and sneak up on prey while hunting

Note: Boldfaced words that are defined in the book may not appear in the glossary.

Index

1 2 3 4 5 6 7 8 9 0 Printed in the U.S.A. 1 0 9 8 7 6 5 4 3 2